I0017306

Table of Contents

Topic Areas

Enterprise Structure and Master Data 11% to 20%

Inventory Management and Physical Inventory 11%-20%

Procurement Processes 11% - 20%

Valuation and Account Assignment <= 10%

Purchasing Optimization <= 10%

Consumption-Based Planning <= 10%

SAP S/4HANA User Experience <= 10%

Configuration of Purchasing <= 10%

Invoice Verification <= 10%

Analytics in Sourcing and Procurement <= 10%

Sources of Supply <= 10%

Managing Clean Core <= 10%

Disclaimer

These questions are for self-evaluation purposes and may or may not appear on the actual certification exams. Answering these questions correctly is no 100% guarantee that you will pass the certification exam. The certification exam covers a much broader spectrum of topics, so do make sure you have familiarized yourself with all topics listed in the exam competency areas before taking the certification exam. But this book will help you in preparation of certification exam.

We are not related to, affiliated with, endorsed or authorized by SAP. Please note that the questions and answers provided are intended for practice purposes only and do not represent actual SAP certification exams or official SAP content.

Use this material at your own responsibility and discretion. It is recommended to consult official SAP documentation and training materials for the most accurate and up-to-date information.

Answering a question correctly results in one point. Answering a question incorrectly results in zero points.

For multiple choice questions, all the responses need to be correct to be awarded one point.

Good Luck!

Description

About Certification

Level	Associate

Exam	80 questions

Cut Score	63%

Duration	180 mins

150+ unique Practice Questions and Answers of **C_TS452_2410** certification.

Questions and Answers

Question:
Which of the following features of self-service procurement in SAP S/4HANA allows users to select and order products from predefined catalogs? Please choose the correct answer.
Response:
Purchase Requisition
Shopping Cart
Purchase Order
Supplier Quotation

Question:
What influences account determination in general ledger accounting? There are 2 correct answers to this question.
Response:
Through the evaluation area
Through the evaluation group
Through the controlling area
Through the chart of accounts

Question:
You intend to procure low-value material over a period of time up to a specific amount. What type of purchasing document is best suited for this purpose? Please choose the correct answer.
Response:
Release purchase order
Blanket purchase order
Service purchase order
Standard purchase order

Question:
What are some key features of the goods-receipt-based (GR-based) invoice verification? There are 3 correct answers to this question.
Response:
The system generates an invoice item for each purchase order item.

As a prerequisite, the indicator for GR-based invoice verification is set in the purchase order item.
Each invoice item is assigned to a goods receipt item.
A goods receipt must be posted prior to the invoice.

Question:
In which cases do you receive an error message from the system if the automatic account determination was set up incorrectly? There are 3 correct answers to this question.
Response:
In case of material price change
In the case of a booking in the goods receipt blocked stock (GR blocked stock)
In the event of a transfer from one inventory type to another
In the event of a transfer from one company code to another

Question:
Which of the following statements apply to manually created reservation? There are 2 correct answers to this question.
Response:
You can assign different account assignments objects per item.
You must enter a material number in the item.
You can maintain different movement types per item.
You can set the movement allowed indicator per item.

Question:
In SAP S/4HANA, which tool provides real-time insights into procurement data through interactive dashboards and visualizations? Please choose the correct answer.
Response:
SAP Fiori Apps
SAP BW/4HANA
SAP Ariba Analytics
SAP Analytics Cloud

Question:

A company wants to provide its employees with a mobile-friendly interface for creating purchase requisitions on the go. Which tool in SAP S/4HANA can support this requirement? There are 2 correct answers to this question.

Response:

SAP Fiori Mobile Apps

SAP Ariba Mobile App

SAP Fieldglass Mobile App

SAP SRM Mobile

Question:

What is included in the functional scope of the purchasing analytics KPI tiles? There are 2 correct answers to this question.

Response:

This includes automatic database updates whenever tile changes occur.

The Smart Business Alert functionality is part of it. Such a Smart Business Alert goes to specific people when a predetermined limit is exceeded.

Smart controls such as SmartChart control and SmartFilterBar control are included.

This includes insight-to-action with drill-down functionality (display of different drill-down levels).

Question:

Which of the following goods issues update the consumption in SAP Materials Management? Please choose the correct answer.

Response:

Cost center

Random sampling

Scrapping

Production order

Question:

Which field selection key is used in combination with a document category in SAP Materials Management? Please choose the correct answer.
Response:
Release status
Item category
Price Display Authorization
Activity category

Question:
Your company wants to automatically convert purchase requisitions into purchase orders for some materials. What must be guaranteed for this? There are 3 correct answers to this question.
Response:
A source of supply with valid conditions is assigned to the purchase requisition.
There is a plant-specific order book entry for the material.
The Automatic order indicator is activated in the master record of the business partner or supplier.
The Automatic order indicator is activated in the material master.

Question:
In which situation can you have open items in the GR/IR clearing account? Please choose the correct answer.
Response:
Price differences between purchase order and invoice receipt for a purchase order item
Price differences at invoice receipt for an order item, only if the material is valuated at the standard price
Price differences at invoice receipt for an order item, only if the material is valuated at the moving average price
Quantity differences between goods receipts and invoice receipts for a purchase order item

Question:

A company wants to ensure that a specific material is always available in stock to meet urgent customer demands. Which feature in SAP S/4HANA can be used to reserve stock for this material? There are 2 correct answers to this question.
Response:
Material Reservation
Stock Transfer
Transfer Posting
Material Safety Stock

Question:
How can you automatically update the pricing conditions in a purchasing info record? Please choose the correct answer.
Response:
Select the Info Update indicator when maintaining a quotation.
Select the Info Update indicator when maintaining a contract.
Select the Info Update indicator when creating a purchase order.
Select the Info Update indicator when creating a contract release order.

Question:
You use quota arrangements. You include a new supplier in an existing quota system. How can you ensure that the new supplier is considered as if they had been part of the quota arrangement from the beginning? Please choose the correct answer.
Response:
Manually update the quota base quantity.
Manually update the quota-allocated quantity.
Manually update the quota.
Manually update the source list.

Question:
Which statements apply to the final delivery indicator in an order item? There are 3 correct answers to this question.
Response:

As soon as it is set, the order item no longer has any significance for requirements planning.
The indicator can be set manually when booking the goods receipt.
If it is set, goods receipt can no longer be posted for the corresponding order item.
It is set automatically by the system if the delivered quantity does not fall below the underdelivery tolerance.

Question:
You transfer material between two plants. The goods issue in the delivery plant is booked. During the transportation process, some parts of the shipment will be damaged, the delivery factory is responsible for the transportation. How can scrapping be booked? Please choose the correct answer.
Response:
You post the goods receipt for the total quantity in the receiving plant to the unrestricted-use inventory and post the scrapping there.
You adjust the stock in transit and store the remaining quantity in the receiving plant. The scrapping is then booked equally in the delivering and receiving plants.
You cancel the stock transfer in the issuing plant and post the scrapping there.
You post the goods receipt for the total quantity in the receiving plant to blocked stock and then scrap the damaged parts there.

Question:
Which of the following is NOT a standard type of goods movement in SAP S/4HANA? Please choose the correct answer.
Response:
Goods Receipt
Goods Issue
Goods Transfer
Goods Return

Question:

In SAP S/4HANA, which transaction is primarily used for goods movement, including goods receipt and goods issue? Please choose the correct answer.

Response:

MIRO

MIGO

ME21N

ME23N

Question:

A goods receipt was posted for an order item. The material has the material type NLAG (non-stock material). What happens? There are 2 correct answers to this question.

Response:

The quantity is posted to a special inventory for non-stock material.

The value is posted to a consumption account.

The value of the material is reduced accordingly in the warehouse.

The quantity is posted to consumption.

Question:

Which of the following is a key benefit of using analytics in sourcing and procurement processes? Please choose the correct answer.

Response:

It eliminates the need for purchase orders.

It provides insights into supplier performance and compliance.

It automates the procurement process.

It replaces the traditional procurement module.

Question:

In which of the following business transactions will you get an error message if you have NOT set up automatic account determination? There are 3 correct answers to this question.

Response:

Goods receipt of valuated material

Material price changes

Goods issue of valuated material
Goods receipt of consignment stock

Question:
What information on the subject of contracts can be accessed
directly via analytical apps? There are 2 correct answers to this
question.
Response:
Asset value contracts
Unapproved Contracts
Expiring contracts
Unused contracts

Question:
What happens when you call transaction MB01 in SAP S/4HANA?
Please choose the correct answer.
Response:
MB01 issues a warning message
MB01 issues an error message
MB01 creates a short dump
MB01 redirects you to transaction BP

Question:
Which of the following are characteristics of the Hold function for
purchase orders? There are 2 correct answers to this question.
Response:
It disables follow-on activities.
It is supported for blanket purchase orders.
It allows any kind of error in a document.
It triggers a workflow to request completion of the document.

Question:
Which field in the material master can be used to prevent materials
from being ordered that are no longer available? Please choose the
correct answer.
Response:

The Expiration indicator field
The Special procurement type field
The Material Status field
The Authorization Group field

Question:
Which of the following occurs when you park a supplier invoice related to a purchase order? There are 2 correct answers to this question.
Response:
An Fl invoice is posted and blocked for payment.
G/L accounts are updated.
The purchase order history is updated.
An MM invoice document is created.

Question:
In SAP S/4HANA, which master data element contains information about which supplier can supply which material under which conditions? Please choose the correct answer.
Response:
Material Master
Vendor Master
Purchase Info Record
Source List

Question:

Question:
What are some of the SAP Fiori user types? There are 3 correct answers to this question.
Response:
Occasional
Developer
Business Partner
Expert

Question:
You have several purchasing info records available for a specific material. Given this, what will happen if a purchase requisition is created manually? Please choose the correct answer.
Response:
The system automatically selects the info record that was created least far in the past.
The system automatically selects the info record that offers the cheapest price
The system shows the user all available info records so that he can select one.
The system automatically selects the info record that was used for the previous purchase requisition.

Question:
Which field selection key is used in conjunction with a document type in SAP MM? Please choose the correct answer.
Response:
Group selection
Movement type
Release status
Document type

Question:
A company receives a shipment of defective materials from a supplier. They want to return these materials and ensure that they are not included in unrestricted stock. Which goods movement type in SAP S/4HANA can be used for this purpose? There are 2 correct answers to this question.
Response:
Goods Return
Goods Issue
Transfer Posting to Blocked Stock
Goods Receipt to Unrestricted Stock

Question:
In SAP S/4HANA, which organizational unit is responsible for procuring materials and services, negotiating conditions of purchase with vendors, and is also responsible for tasks relating to invoice verification? Please choose the correct answer.
Response:
Plant
Purchasing Organization
Company Code
Storage Location

Question:
Which of the following is mandatory to create a plant in SAP Materials Management? Please choose the correct answer.
Response:
Tax code
Language key
Local currency
Division

Question:
In SAP S/4HANA, which of the following stock types is considered available for unrestricted use? Please choose the correct answer.
Response:
Unrestricted Stock
Quality Inspection Stock
Blocked Stock
Returns Stock

Question:
A company wants to ensure that employees can only order IT equipment from a list of approved products and suppliers. Which feature in SAP S/4HANA can be used to set up this approved list? There are 2 correct answers to this question.
Response:
Purchase Info Record

Catalog Management
Material Master
Source List

Question:
Which indicator can you set for the manual source assignment in the function authorizations for buyers user parameter (EFB) in SAP Materials Management? Please choose the correct answer.
Response:
Purchase Requisition
Contract
Source List
Quotation

Question:
Your purchasing organization has entered into a contractual agreement with a supplier to purchase 10000 units of a particular material. You have stored this agreement as a quantity contract. How can you prevent a release order in excess of the target quantity? Please choose the correct answer.
Response:
If the order quantity exceeds the target quantity, a warning message is issued. You can set this as an error message in Customizing to prevent release.
You must implement a BADI to check the target quantity in the contract release order and prevent release if the quantity exceeds it.
The system prevents exceeding the target quantity in a release order. NO additional action is required from you.
If the order quantity exceeds the target quantity, a dialog box opens. You can use a special authorization to control whether the user may order the excess quantity.

Question:
A global company wants to consolidate its purchases to achieve better pricing from suppliers. Which of the following features in

SAP S/4HANA can support this initiative? There are 3 correct answers to this question.
Response:
Central Purchasing
Contract Management
Source List
Purchase Requisition Consolidation

Question:
Which of the following movement types in SAP S/4HANA indicates a goods receipt for a purchase order? Please choose the correct answer.
Response:
101
261
341
561

Question:
For which of the following document categories can you perform an item-wise release in the flexible workflow for purchasing? Please choose the correct answer.
Response:
Scheduling agreement
Purchase order
Request for quotation
Purchase requisition

Question:
A company frequently procures a material in bulk and wants to negotiate special prices and conditions with suppliers. Which source of supply in SAP S/4HANA can be used to establish these negotiated terms? There are 2 correct answers to this question.
Response:
Contract
Quotation

Purchase Info Record
Outline Agreement

Question:
When using a classic release procedure, for which of the following documents must you use classification? There are 2 correct answers to this question.
Response:
Requests for quotation
Purchase requisitions
JIT delivery schedules
Purchase orders

Question:
Which of the following is a key benefit of implementing self-service procurement in SAP S/4HANA? Please choose the correct answer.
Response:
It eliminates the need for purchase orders.
It allows for direct communication with suppliers.
It reduces the procurement cycle time by enabling end users to initiate the procurement process.
It replaces the traditional procurement module.

Question:
Which of the following is NOT a key component of source determination in SAP S/4HANA? Please choose the correct answer.
Response:
Quota Arrangement
Source List
Purchase Info Record
Payment Terms

Question:
What does the item category specify in a purchasing document in SAP Materials Management? Please choose the correct answer.

Response:
Whether items with unlimited deliveries are possible
Whether items without a material number are possible
Whether items with order acknowledgment are possible
Whether items without valuation are possible

Question:
What do you have to do to configure an account determination that groups different material types on the same account? Please choose the correct answer.
Response:
The relevant material types are assigned the same evaluation grouping.
The relevant material types are assigned the same evaluation class.
The same account modification is assigned to the relevant material types
The same account class reference is assigned to the relevant material types.

Question:
Which of the following SAP Fiori apps must you use to set up the following Situation Handling use case: Quantity Deficit in Supplier Delivery? There are 2 correct answers to this question.
Response:
Manage Situation Types - Message Based
Manage Teams and Responsibilities
Monitor Situations
Manage Situation Types

Question:
Which of the following is NOT a benefit of optimizing the purchasing process in SAP S/4HANA? Please choose the correct answer.
Response:
Reduced lead times
Increased stock levels

Improved supplier relationships
Cost savings

Question:
Which influencing factors can you use to define field attributes for
a business partner? There are 3 correct answers to this question.
Response:
Account group
Activity
Client
Business partner role

Question:
A company has multiple plants and wants to ensure that specific
materials are only procured by certain plants from approved
suppliers. Which master data element in SAP S/4HANA can help
enforce this? There are 3 correct answers to this question.
Response:
Source List
Material Master - Plant View
Purchase Info Record
Quota Arrangement

Question:
How can a material be blocked for purchasing for a specific plant?
There are 2 correct answers to this question.
Response:
**By using a corresponding plant-specific material status in the
material master**
By entering zero in the Quantity field in the quotation
Through a corresponding blocking note in the supplier master
record
By making a corresponding entry in the order book

Question:

Which of the following tools in SAP S/4HANA allows for the personalization and simplification of traditional SAP GUI screens? Please choose the correct answer.

Response:

SAP Fiori Apps

SAP Fiori Elements

SAP UI5

SAP Screen Personas

Question:

For a material subject to split valuation, at which level is the price control moving average set in SAP Materials Management? Please choose the correct answer.

Response:

Valuation group

Account modification

Account group

Valuation area

Question:

During an inventory, your warehouse manager decided to recount the material inventory for an inventory document. How does a recount take place in the system? Please choose the correct answer.

Response:

A new inventory document is created, and the new counted quantity is recorded with it. If the inventory difference is now posted, the inventory documents for the affected material that still need to be posted will be deleted.

A new inventory document is created with reference to the original document. At the end of the recount, the inventory difference of the original document is first posted and then balanced with the inventory difference of the new document. The difference is posted to an inventory difference account.

The recount quantity is recorded in the existing inventory document and the inventory difference is posted.

A new inventory document is created with reference to the original document. The new counted quantity is now recorded in the new inventory document and the inventory difference is posted.

Question:
How does SAP Fiori achieve the role-based design principle? There are 2 correct answers to this question.
Response:
End users get all the information and functions they need for their daily work, but nothing more.
Navigation, personalization, and application configuration are limited to ensure consistency across user roles.
Single complex transactions are decomposed into several discrete apps suited to the user role.
The application interface adapts to the size and device used by the user.

Question:
What are the different types of SAP Fiori applications? There are 3 correct answers to this question.
Response:
Transactional
Responsive
Factsheet
Analytical

Question:
In the context of invoice verification in SAP S/4HANA, what does the term GR/IR stand for? Please choose the correct answer.
Response:
Goods Receipt/Invoice Receipt
Goods Return/Invoice Return
General Receipt/Invoice Receipt
General Return/Invoice Return

Question:
You want to collectively convert assigned purchase requisitions into purchase orders. What functions can you use? There are 3 correct answers to this question.
Response:
Use the source list.
Run the automatic generation of purchase orders.
Use the assignment list.
Use the document overview in the Create Purchase Order app (ME21N).

Question:
You will receive an invoice from your supplier for a material amounting to €1,000 per 100 pieces. After entering the header data and the order number, the system suggests an invoice amount of €700 and the quantity of 70 pieces from the goods receipt booking. How can you enter the invoice without invoice blocking? There are 2 correct answers to this question.
Response:
Before posting, you define a tolerance group in your user role whose threshold value is not exceeded by the existing deviation. If you do not have the appropriate permission, you must have your system administrator make this role change.
Before you post the invoice, change the Invoice Block indicator in the invoice header to Manually released for payment.
You switch to Park incoming invoice and save the invoice.
You use manual invoice reduction. Select the Supplier Error: Reduce Quantity option and enter the quantity and value on the invoice next to the suggested quantity and value.

Question:
Which object uses an access sequence for message determination? Please choose the correct answer.
Response:
The output device of a message condition record
The message type in a message schema

The message condition set

The message schema of a document type

Question:
In SAP S/4HANA, which valuation method values stock based on the most recent purchase price? Please choose the correct answer.
Response:
Standard Price
Moving Average Price
FIFO
LIFO

Question:
What are the capabilities of Operational Contract Management in SAP S/4HANA? There are 2 correct answers to this question.
Response:
Direct navigation to contract and supplier object pages
Single-screen transactions
Dynamic and flexible search across the entire contract worklist
Fast change option in documents

Question:
Which batch input session accepts data from an external system into SAP Materials Management? Please choose the correct answer.
Response:
Enter count without reference and posting of difference.
Create physical inventory documents.
Block material and freeze book inventory in physical inventory documents.
Set Zero Count indicator in physical inventory documents.

Question:
Which of the following master data elements in SAP S/4HANA provides an overview of all the materials that a company can procure, produce, store, or sell? Please choose the correct answer.
Response:

Material Master
Vendor Master
Purchase Info Record
Source List

Question:
With which field do you control the creation of a scheduling agreement with release documentation? Please choose the correct answer.
Response:
Item Category
Document Type
Release Creation Profile
JIT Indicator

Question:
How does the system derive the company code when you post a goods movement in a plant? Please choose the correct answer.
Response:
A plant can occur several times in a client, but can only belong to one company code.
The company code is derived from your default settings.
A plant is unique in a client, and can only belong to one company code.
Each plant is assigned to a purchasing organization, which itself belongs to one company code.

Question:
Tolerance groups can be defined to post inventory differences. Which tolerances can be defined? There are 2 correct answers to this question.
Response:
Maximum percentage deviation for each inventory difference item
Maximum difference for each inventory document
Maximum absolute deviation for each inventory document line
Maximum difference for each inventory document line

Question:
What personalization options do you have for the Fiori Launchpad?
Please select 3 correct answers that apply.
Response:
You can add tiles to existing tile groups.
You can move a tile to another tile group.
You can add new catalogs.
You can remove tiles from a tile group.

Question:
Where do you enable the ability to personalize the home page?
Please choose the correct answer.
Response:
In the configuration of the SAP Fiori launchpad
In the user settings in the back-end system
In the business catalog
In the business role assigned to the user

Question:
What does the system use to determine a source of supply? Please
choose the correct answer.
Response:
Purchase requisitions
Requests for quotation
Purchase contracts
Purchasing info records

Question:
Which of the following are valid sources of supply in a source list
in SAP Materials Management? There are 2 correct answers to this
question.
Response:
Quota arrangement
Quotation

Contract
Procurement plant

Question:
What are the requirements for using flexible order approval
(flexible order approval workflow)? There are 3 correct answers to
this question.
Response:
Setting the prerequisites for the flexible workflow in the
Manage Order Workflows app
Determining the recipients for the flexible workflow in the
Manage Order Workflows app
Activation of Flexible Workflow for Orders in Customizing
Deactivation of the classic release process

Question:
You want to create a purchase order. An info record is available for
the material-supplier combination. What logic does the system use
to determine a price from the info record? There are 2 correct
answers to this question.
Response:
The system always proposes the price from the last purchase order,
if available.
The system always proposes the valid plant-specific price, if
available.
The system always proposes the price stored at purchasing
organization level, if available.
If there are NO valid conditions, the system can propose the
price from the last purchase order, if available.

Question:
What happens when you post a logistics invoice for a purchase
order that you have received in the system? There are 2 correct
answers to this question.
Response:
The payment is posted against open liabilities.

The accounting documents are created.
The purchase order history is updated.
Open liabilities are evaluated.

Question:
How can you prevent a release order from being created in excess of the target quantity of a quantity contract? Please choose the correct answer.

Response:

If the order quantity exceeds the target quantity, a warning message is issued. You can set this as an error message in Customizing to prevent release

You must implement a BADI to check the target quantity in the contract release order and prevent release if the quantity exceeds it.

The system prevents exceeding the target quantity in a release order. NO additional action is required from you.

If the order quantity exceeds the target quantity, a dialog box opens. You can use a special authorization to control whether the user may order the excess quantity.

Question:
In consumption-based planning, which of the following lot-sizing procedures determines the order quantity by considering the net requirements within a given period? Please choose the correct answer.

Response:

Lot-for-lot order quantity

Fixed lot size

Period lot size

Replenishment up to maximum stock level

Question:
How can an open item arise on the WE/RE account? Please choose the correct answer.

Response:

Due to price deviations within the goods receipt document that arise from the valuation based on the moving average price

Due to price deviations within the goods receipt document that arise from the valuation based on the standard price

Due to quantity deviations of certain items between goods receipt and invoice

Due to price deviations of certain items between the order and the invoice

You enter a supplier invoice for a purchase order that has already been delivered. Apart from the purchase order number itself, what information can you use as a reference? There are 2 correct answers to this question.

Response:

Bill of lading number

Inbound delivery number

Material document number

Delivery note number

Question:

Confirmed quantities and delivery dates are recorded in the order items, and your company requires order confirmations and shipping notifications from all suppliers. Which settings are necessary for this? Please choose the correct answer.

Response:

A confirmation control key marked as Relevant to ASN.

A confirmation control key that contains a sequence of two confirmation types.

A confirmation control key that contains at least one confirmation type marked as relevant to planning

A purchase confirmation key in which the Order Confirmation indicator is set

Question:

What is typical for a position type in purchasing? Please choose the correct answer.
Response:
The selection of item categories in a purchase order document depends on the account assignment category.
The item category to be selected influences a planning run in FI.
You can assign a field selection key to the item category in Customizing.
The selection of item categories in an order document depends on the order type.

Question:
Which SAP Smart Business KPIs are available in connection with purchase requisitions? There are 3 correct answers to this question.
Response:
Average approval time for purchase requisition
Cycle time from purchase requisition to purchase order
Order requisition processing effort
Overdue purchase requisition items

Question:
Which of the following actions can you run with transact on MIGO? There are 3 correct answers to this question.
Response:
Cancel material document
Enter physical inventory count
Release GR blocked stock
Create return delivery

Question:
A company wants to ensure that all purchase requisitions created through self-service procurement undergo a managerial approval process. Which feature in SAP S/4HANA can be configured to enforce this requirement? There are 2 correct answers to this question.
Response:

Release Strategy
Workflow Configuration
Catalog Management
Purchase Order Type

Question:
What do you need to consider when deciding whether to use stock transport orders for stock transfers between plants? Please choose the correct answer.
Response:
Stock transfers with stock transport orders can be integrated with MRP
Stock transfers with transport orders are one step only
Stock transfers with stock transport orders require an account assignment
Stock transfers with stock transport orders use the same calculation schema as standard purchase orders

Question:
What adjustments (personalization) can be made to the Fiori Launchpad? There are 2 correct answers to this question.
Response:
Choice of design theme
Choice of Fiori version
Language and region specific settings
Choice of tile size (small, medium, large)

Question:
In SAP S/4HANA, which feature allows for the automatic determination of potential sources of supply during the procurement process? Please choose the correct answer.
Response:
Source Determination
Supplier Evaluation
Quota Arrangement
Purchase Order Management

Question:
You send newly created purchase orders to a supplier via email, whereas quantity or price changes are to be transmitted by fax. What prerequisites must be met? There are 3 correct answers to this question.
Response:
The Exclusive indicator is flagged in the access sequence.
The condition record contains the Price and Quantity fields.
The New Message Determination Process for Change Messages indicator is flagged in Customizing.
The Price and Quantity fields are relevant for printout changes.

Question:
Which of the following tools in SAP S/4HANA can be used to determine the best source of supply for a material based on certain criteria? Please choose the correct answer.
Response:
Source Determination
Supplier Evaluation
Quota Arrangement
Purchase Order Management

Question:
In the company code for which you are responsible, a separate purchasing organization is required for each plant. What do you need to consider when creating the organizational structure? There are 2 correct answers to this question.
Response:
That each purchasing organization has its own vendor master records (supplier master records).
That each purchasing organization has its own purchasing groups
That each purchasing organization has its own information records
That each purchasing organization has its own material masters

Question:
To which stock types can you post a goods receipt without referencing a purchase order or a production order? There are 3 correct answers to this question.
Response:
Unrestricted-use stock
Valuated GR blocked stock
Blocked stock
Quality inspection stock

Question:
What requirements must be met so that the system checks the best-before date in the order when goods are received? There are 3 correct answers to this question.
Response:
The minimum durability check is activated for the movement type.
The storage location for the material to be stored is determined via Warehouse Management.
The remaining shelf life is maintained in the order data.
The minimum durability test is activated for the plant.

Question:
You are posting a goods receipt without a corresponding purchase order (PO) in the system. Which of the following are prerequisites for automatic generation of the PO at the time of goods receipt? There are 3 correct answers to this question.
Response:
The delivered material is a valuated stock material.
The goods receipt to be posted is intended for consumption.
Automatic purchase order generation is activated for the movement type in Customizing.
A valid purchasing info record exists for the material and supplier combination.

Question:

Which of the following prerequisites must be met for the system to check the shelf life of materials at goods receipt? There are 3 correct answers to this question.
Response:
The purchase order item contains the remaining shelf life.
The shelf life expiration date check is activated for the material type in Customizing.
The shelf life expiration date check is activated for the movement type in Customizing.
The shelf life expiration date check is activated for the plant in Customizing.

Question:
At which of the following organizational levels must you maintain a business partner master record for a supplier? There are 3 correct answers to this question.
Response:
Purchasing organization
Plant
Company code
Client

Question:
Which of the following are possible personalization options of the SAP Fiori launchpad? There are 2 correct answers to this question.
Response:
Settings for language and region
Selection of the design theme
Selection of tile size
Selection of an SAP fiori catalog

Question:
Which statements apply to delivery plans? There are 3 correct answers to this question.
Response:

Scheduling agreement items do not have to contain material master records
Delivery plans are always assigned to a specific plant.
Delivery plans can be used for consignment processes (shipment processes).
Delivery plans can only be created manually.

Question:
You regularly purchase non-stock materials. What must you set up to allow the system to automatically propose specific accounts?
Please choose the correct answer.
Response:
Assign valuation classes to the account assignment categories.
Assign valuation classes to the material groups.
Assign transaction keys to the account assignment categories.
Assign transaction keys to the material groups

Question:
Where do you encounter postings with automatic account determination in materials management? There are 3 correct answers to this question.
Response:
In purchase requisitions
In material evaluation
In inventory management
In the inventory check

Question:
Which assignments are essential for external procurement? Please choose the correct answer.
Response:
Business area - purchasing organization
Reference purchasing organization - purchasing organization
Plant - purchasing organization
Company code - purchasing organization

Question:
Which of the following tools in SAP S/4HANA provides a runtime and development environment for web-based applications? Please choose the correct answer.
Response:
SAP Fiori Launchpad
SAP Fiori Elements
SAP UI5
SAP Screen Personas

Question:
Which statements apply to the final delivery indicator in an order item? There are 3 correct answers to this question.
Response:
As soon as it is set, the order item no longer has any significance for requirements planning.
The indicator can be set manually when booking the goods receipt.
If it is set, goods receipt can no longer be posted for the corresponding order item.
It is set automatically by the system if the delivered quantity does not fall below the underdelivery tolerance.

Question:
A multinational company operates in multiple countries and wants to maintain different terms of payment, currencies, and tax regulations for a single supplier. Which feature in SAP S/4HANA allows for this differentiation? There are 2 correct answers to this question.
Response:
Vendor Subrange
Vendor Master - Purchasing View
Vendor Master - Company Code View
Purchase Info Record

Question:
What do you have to set so that price conditions in orders are only visible to certain users? Please choose the correct answer.
Response:
The transaction field selection key
The activity category field selection key
The user parameters EVO
The user parameters EFB

Question:
Which of the following are possible personalization options of the SAP Fiori launchpad? There are 2 correct answers to this question.
Response:
Add tiles to existing tile groups.
Add new tile groups.
Add tile groups to business roles.
Add new catalogs.

Question:
Where can you maintain purchasing conditions in SAP Materials Management? There are 3 correct answers to this question.
Response:
Purchase requisitions
Outline agreements
Info records
Quotations

Question:
In the context of analytics in sourcing and procurement, which feature in SAP S/4HANA provides a comprehensive view of all procurement activities, including purchase orders, contracts, and supplier evaluations? Please choose the correct answer.
Response:
Procurement Overview Page
Supplier Evaluation Dashboard
Spend Analysis Report

Purchase Order Analytics

Question:
Which of the following assignments can you configure? There are 2 correct answers to this question.
Response:
The allowed item categories for each account assignment category.
The allowed account assignment categories for each item category.
The allowed account assignment categories for each document type.
The allowed item categories for each document type.

Question:
You are interested in the percentage of shopping cart items that require manual changes to either the PO or the PR after initial creation and approval. What key performance indicator (KPI) proceeds the information? Please choose the correct answer.
Response:
PR Low Touch Rate
PR High Touch Rate
PR to Order Cycle time
PR item changes

Question:
A company has a policy to hold payment for invoices that have a price variance beyond a certain threshold. Which configuration element in SAP S/4HANA can be set up to automatically block such invoices for payment? There are 2 correct answers to this question.
Response:
Tolerance Key
Payment Terms
Release Strategy
Invoice Block Key

Question:

What does the system do during reorder point planning? There are 3 correct answers to this question.
Response:
It performs backward scheduling to determine the availability dates of the purchase requisitions.
It recalculates the replenishment lead time for materials with automatic reorder point planning
It performs a net requirements calculation for each material that is part of the planning run.
It performs a lot size calculation for each material with net requirements.

Question:
Which of the following capabilities does the end-to-end Operational Procurement solution in SAP S/4HANA provide? There are 3 correct answers to this question.
Response:
Service purchasing
Spend visibility
Self-service requisitioning
Purchase order collaboration

Question:
A company has received a shipment of goods but notices that some items are damaged. Which document should they create in SAP S/4HANA to record the discrepancy? There are 2 correct answers to this question.
Response:
Goods Receipt
Return Delivery
Purchase Order
Purchase Requisition

Question:
Which of the following is NOT a standard procurement process in SAP S/4HANA? Please choose the correct answer.

Response:
Purchase Requisition
Purchase Order
Sales Order
Goods Receipt

Question:
A company is implementing a new procurement process to improve
efficiency. They want to ensure that all purchase requisitions are
approved by a manager before a purchase order is created. Which
of the following steps should be included in their process? Please
select 3 correct answers that apply.
Response:
Create Purchase Requisition
Manager Approval
Create Sales Order
Create Purchase Order

Question:
Which work steps can be part of the contract processing process?
There are 3 correct answers to this question.
Response:
The subsequent booking of component consumption
**The purchase of components that are delivered directly to the
subcontractor**
Creating an outbound delivery for materials that are to be made
available to the subcontractor
The billing of component consumption by the subcontractor

Question:
Which principle of SAP Fiori realizes the idea of ONE user per use
case with up to three screens per application? Please choose the
correct answer.
Response:
The principle of role base
The principle of simplicity

The principle of cloud design
The principle of corporate design

Question:
Which of the following attributes can you maintain in an account assignment category in SAP Materials Management? There are 3 correct answers to this question.
Response:
Account modification
Consumption posting
Message output parameter
Special stock

Question:
Which user interface in SAP S/4HANA provides a role-based, personalized, and intuitive experience across various devices and deployment options? Please choose the correct answer.
Response:
SAP GUI
SAP Fiori
SAP Web Dynpro
SAP NetWeaver Portal

Question:
Where in SAP MM can you find automatic account determination? Please choose the correct answer.
Response:
When creating purchase requisitions
When evaluating materials
In inventory management
In auditing

Question:
What must you consider when defining purchasing organizations? There are 3 correct answers to this question.
Response:

Each purchasing organization has its own material master data.
Each purchasing organization has its own info records.
Each purchasing organization has its own supplier master data.
Each purchasing organization has its own purchasing groups.

Question:
In which of the following cases does an open item OP arise on the GR/IR clearing account? There are 2 correct answers to this question.
Response:
The quantity for an order item in the order is greater than the quantity actually delivered.
The invoiced quantity for an order item is greater than the quantity actually delivered.
The actual quantity delivered for an order item is greater than the invoiced quantity
The quantity for an order item is larger in the order than in the invoice.

Question:
Which assignment must NOT be established if you plan to set up a cross-company purchasing organization? Please choose the correct answer.
Response:
Purchasing group - factory
Purchasing organization - plant
Purchasing organization - company code
Purchasing group - company code

Question:
What data does the system require to determine the safety stock during automatic reorder point planning? There are 3 correct answers to this question.
Response:
The storage costs code
Mean absolute deviation

Replenishment lead time
Service level

Question:
How often does SAP HANA create a save point? Please choose the correct answer.
Response:
Every few minutes
Every few seconds
Every few hours
Every 30 minutes

Question:
For which of the following functions is sourcing available? There are 2 correct answers to this question.
Response:
Conversion of a planned order into a purchase requisition
Creating a contract release
Assignment and processing of purchase requisitions
Creating a collective call with delivery allocations based on percentage points

Question:
In SAP S/4HANA, which of the following can be used to post an invoice for a partial delivery? Please choose the correct answer.
Response:
Invoice Reduction
Subsequent Debit
Subsequent Credit
Invoice Parking

Question:
For which documents do you have to use the classification if you want to use the classic release procedure? There are 2 correct answers to this question.
Response:

Fine retrieval (just-in-time retrieval)
Supplier inquiry
Order
Purchase Requirements

Question:
At which organizational do you assign release creation profiles for scheduling agreement within a Business Partner? Please choose the correct answer.
Response:
Purchase organization
Plant
Company code
Client

Question:
You convert a purchase requisition to a purchase order. What can you assign to the purchase requisition to be used as a source of supply? There are 2 correct answers to this question.
Response:
Desired vendor
Quota arrangement
Info record
Contract

Question:
What characterizes the role-based structure of SAP Fiori? There are 3 correct answers to this question.
Response:
Transactions are broken down into small units and assigned to specific user roles according to the users needs
Fiori provides the right data at the right time.
The user receives exactly what he needs for his work area.
The user can adapt apps according to their needs.

Question:

When purchasing externally, how can you prevent the purchase of materials that have no longer been valid? Please choose the correct answer.
Response:
By activating a supplier block
By setting the material to Inactive.
By setting the procurement type to Internal administration only.
By activating the corresponding material status.

Question:
What characterizes goods receipt-related invoice verification?
There are 3 correct answers to this question.
Response:
The indicator for goods receipt-related invoice verification must have been set in advance in the respective order items
A separate invoice is generated for each order item.
The goods receipt is posted before the invoice.
Each invoice item is assigned to a goods receipt item

Question:
In which transaction can you view stock overview in SAP S/4HANA? Please choose the correct answer.
Response:
ME23N
MMBE
MI01
VA03

Question:
What advantage does the submission number offer in supplier inquiries? Please choose the correct answer.
Response:
The submission number makes it easier to select offers for price comparison.
Submission numbers make it easier to find discount surcharges.

The submission number makes it easier to select documents from the offers for creating order book entries.
The submission number makes it easier to select documents for generating RFP reports.

Question:
Which SAP Fiori design principle has the goal of having one user. one use case, and up to three screens for each application? Please choose the correct answer.
Response:
Simple
Responsive
Role-based
Instant value

Question:
What information does the Purchasing Group Activities analysis app provide? There are 2 correct answers to this question.
Response:
The number of orders and purchase requisitions per buyer and month in the current year
The number of disputed deliveries per buyer in the current year
The number of contracts per purchasing group in the current year
The net purchase value (net order amount) per purchasing group and month in the current year

Question:
Which of the following information can be used as a reference when posting an invoice if goods have already been received for the corresponding order? There are 3 correct answers to this question.
Response:
The purchase requisition number
The waybill number
The delivery note number
The order number

Question:
Which of the following sources of supply in SAP S/4HANA is a framework agreement between a supplier and a purchasing organization that does not contain details of the delivery dates? Please choose the correct answer.
Response:
Purchase Order
Contract
Quotation
Scheduling Agreement

Question:
In SAP S/4HANA, which master data element provides a link between a material and a supplier, indicating that the material can be procured from that supplier? Please choose the correct answer.
Response:
Material Master
Vendor Master
Purchase Info Record
Source List

Question:
Which maintenance statuses must be defined in SAP Materials Management before you buy a valued material for receipt into stock? There are 2 correct answers to this question.
Response:
Accounting
Storage
Costing
Purchasing

Question:
Which statements apply to roles? There are 3 correct answers to this question.
Response:

Role profiles can be created manually.

Roles limit the user radius of action in the system.

To create role profiles, you must use the role management functions (transaction PFCG).

Roles can contain transactions.

Question:

Which of the following analytics tools in SAP S/4HANA provides a cloud-based platform for data connectivity, visualization, and sharing insights? Please choose the correct answer.

Response:

SAP Fiori Apps

SAP BW/4HANA

SAP Ariba Analytics

SAP Analytics Cloud

Question:

In which of the following situations can document parking be used? There are 2 correct answers to this question.

Account assignment information is missing for an invoice item.

A goods receipt is posted for an item that needs a quality inspection.

An EDI invoice is received containing variances.

Account assignment information is missing for a purchase order item.

Question:

Which transfer postings within a plant result in both a material document and an accounting document in SAP Materials Management? There are 2 correct answers to this question.

A material-to-material transfer posting

A transfer posting from one storage location to another storage location

A transfer posting from consignment stock into own stock

A transfer posting from quality inspection stock into unrestricted-use stock

Question:
You posted a goods receipt at origin acceptance in SAP Materials Management. For which stock type is the inventory updated? Please choose the correct answer.
Non-valuated GR blocked stock
Blocked stock
Valuated GR blocked stock
Unrestricted-use stock

Question:
In what ways can you personalize the Procurement Overview page in SAP S/4HANA? There are 3 correct answers to this question.
Extend the set with a new card.
Hide an existing card.
Change the position of cards.
Filter information on a card.

Question:
A supplier regularly supplies your company's warehouse with a specific material. However, a payment liability only arises at the moment you remove the material there. What do you call this procurement process? Please choose the correct answer.
Rearrangement
Quota order
Consignment
Route processing

Question:
What applies to the WORK object? Please choose the correct answer.
A plant can only be assigned to one purchasing organization.
A plant can be assigned to one or more companies.
One or more purchasing organizations can be assigned to a plant.
A plant can only be assigned to one controlling area.

Question:
Which document type in SAP Materials Management triggers automatic sourcing for externally procured materials? Please choose the correct answer.

Scheduling agreement

Request for quotation

Purchase requisition

Contract

All the Best!

www.ingramcontent.com/pod-product-compliance
Lightning Source LLC
LaVergne TN
LVHW051622050326
832903LV00033B/4615